Moths

by Helen Frost

Consulting Editor: Gail Saunders-Smith, Ph.D.

Consultant: Gary A. Dunn, Director of Education,
Young Entomologists' Society

Pebble Books

an imprint of Capstone Press
Mankato, Minnesota

Pebble Books are published by Capstone Press
151 Good Counsel Drive, P.O. Box 669, Mankato, Minnesota 56002
http://www.capstone-press.com

1 2 3 4 5 6 06 05 04 03 02 01

Library of Congress Cataloging-in-Publication Data
Frost, Helen, 1949–
    Moths/by Helen Frost.
    p. cm.—(Insects)
    Includes bibliographical references (p. 23) and index.
    ISBN 0-7368-0852-3
    1. Moths—Juvenile literature. [1. Moths.] I. Title. II. Insects (Mankato, Minn.)
QL544.2 .F77 2001
595.78—dc21   00-009677

Summary: Simple text and photographs describe the physical characteristics and habits of moths.

Note to Parents and Teachers

The Insects series supports national science standards on units on the diversity and unity of life. The series shows that animals have features that help them live in different environments. This book describes moths and illustrates their parts and habits. The photographs support early readers in understanding the text. The repetition of words and phrases helps early readers learn new words. This book also introduces early readers to subject-specific vocabulary words, which are defined in the Words to Know section. Early readers may need assistance to read some words and to use the Table of Contents, Words to Know, Read More, Internet Sites, and Index/Word List sections of the book.

Table of Contents

4

Most moths have
big, hairy bodies.

cecropia moth

Most moths
are dull colors.

great ash sphinx moth

antennas

8

Most moths have antennas that look like feathers.

luna moth

proboscis

Most moths use
a proboscis to drink
plant juices.

white-lined sphinx moth

Most moths have
four wings.

cecropia moth

14

Most moths rest with their wings down.

Mexican tiger moth

eyespots

Some moths have
eyespots on their wings
to scare predators.

io moth

Many moths hide in
trees during the day.

big poplar sphinx moth

Many moths fly
toward light at night.

polyphemus moths

21

Words to Know

antenna—a feeler on an insect's head

dull—not bright or colorful; many moths are dull colors such as gray and brown; most butterflies are bright colors.

eyespots—spots on an insect's wings that look like the eyes of a larger animal; eyespots may scare predators.

moth—an insect similar to a butterfly; more than 100,000 kinds of moths live in the world.

predator—an animal that hunts and eats other animals; birds, spiders, frogs, and bats are predators of moths.

proboscis—a long, tube-shaped mouthpart; moths use their proboscis to drink plant juices.

wing—a movable part of an insect that helps it fly

Read More

Brimner, Larry Dane. *Butterflies and Moths.* A True Book. New York: Children's Press, 1999.

Kottke, Jan. *From Caterpillar to Moth.* How Things Grow. New York: Children's Press, 2000.

Pascoe, Elaine. *Butterflies and Moths.* Nature Close-up. Woodbridge, Conn.: Blackbirch Press, 1997.

Richardson, Adele D. *Moths.* Bugs. Mankato, Minn.: Smart Apple Media, 1999.

Internet Sites

Butterfly or Moth?
http://www.EnchantedLearning.com/subjects/butterfly/allabout/Bflyormoth.shtml

Cecropia Moth—Life Cycle
http://www.geocities.com/RainForest/5479/index.html

Moths of North America
http://www.npwrc.usgs.gov/resource/distr/lepid/moths/mothsusa.htm

Index/Word List

Word Count: 65
Early-Intervention Level: 7

Editorial Credits

Mari C. Schuh, editor; Timothy Halldin, cover designer; Kia Bielke, production
  designer; Kimberly Danger, photo researcher

Photo Credits

Bill Beatty, 16
David Liebman, 20
Dwight R. Kuhn, 8
GeoIMAGERY/Russell Burden, 4, 12; Bruce D. Flaig, 10
John S. Reid, 14
Visuals Unlimited/Leroy Simon, cover; Mark A. Schneider, 1;
  Rob & Ann Simpson, 6, 18